Grace in depression

From the series:

Games of masquerade and walls of doubt

People, systems and mental health at a London university

David Wong

Grace in depression

Series: Games of masquerade and walls of doubt
People, systems and mental health at a London university

David Wong

ISBN: 978-1-7397670-2-0 paperback
        978-1-7397670-3-7 ebook

Copyright © 2025 David Wong

Contact: games6wallsbt@gmail.com

Published by Fountain Framework Publishing, London
https://fountaindiscover.click/

Internet resources were last accessed in April 2024.

Contents

What is grace?..5

Depression from the get-go...8

The denial..9

Mind over actions... 13

The Grace Moment... 14

Is it fair? 17

Hearing voices and multiple selves................................... 19

The essence of grace 22

Who is grace?... 25

Going forward.. 32

What about church? 37

Open door church 45

Your turn 51

References.. 53

What is grace?

Grace is one of the unusual words when we probably use it to mean something beautiful and pleasant, and rarely to anything except persons.

To invoke grace along with depression is a deeply troubling move. The extremities of the two words become even more extreme when placed next to each other. However, that is my full intention. There is much to understand about the idea of "grace in depression", but it will be thoroughly worth our effort to find out more about each of their meanings. Also, this is the situation I have been in for some months, and I hope it will remain with me for years to come.

I take the biblical meaning of grace. As an introduction, the old-time tune "Amazing Grace"[1] has three contrasting words in the first two lines of the lyrics: "sweet", "wretch", and "saved".

---

[1] https://hymnary.org/text/amazing_grace_how_sweet_the_sound

Within such a small space, the words compete for our attention. One of them will triumph over the others.

Amazing Grace,
how sweet the sound
That saved a wretch like me.

Looking deeper, I see that the same grace that is sweet also saved a wretch, being the songwriter John Newton.[2] During his younger days, Newton was a sailor, leading a way of life on the sea and slave trading that even other sailors of the time considered beyond unsavoury and rude.

A master at sea, Newton was so exhausted during a storm in 1748 that he gave up steering. With time to think, he recalled his mother and what words she had used from the Bible to teach him. He began a journey of returning to God. In the early

---

[2] https://www.britannica.com/biography/John-Newton, https://cowperandnewtonmuseum.org.uk/amazing-grace/ and https://rlo.acton.org/archives/124988-john-newton-from-slave-trader-to-abolitionist-pastor.html

1770s, he wrote "Faith's review and expectation (Amazing Grace)", which was published a few years later. Today, we know it as "Amazing Grace".

Whether Newton suffered from depression history does not tell us. The word "depression" is not likely used in the same way in those days. However, a close friend of Newton, William Cowper, had been described as someone who experienced depression much of his life. Today, "Amazing Grace" is a central tenet for many depression sufferers to help them cope.

I have not been lost at sea as Newton experienced, or the kind of fear Cowper experienced that cast him to an insane asylum, further suicidal attempts, and eventually led to his death by despair. What is common is that our actions go hand in hand with our thoughts. Most of us can attest that we can control our minds: we tell ourselves we can stay longer in bed because it's a Saturday. We don't need to go to work, or we convince ourselves that we can go to the shop tomorrow rather than rushing there now, and that the item we want will remain on the shelf!

Depression from the get-go

The first account of depression could well be that experienced by Adam and Eve, when they hid themselves from God because they had done something really naughty. (Genesis 3) They knew it was a bad move, especially since they could not undo it. It was a bad action because God said it would be for such an action. In his self-defence, Adam dissociated the product (apple) from the action (eating). However, there was far more evidence against him and Eve. What substance their defence barristers and artificial intelligence chatbots had for them stood them no chance to change the law that stipulated that the eating of the fruit from that tree is forbidden.

Hannah and Samson are two further examples. Hannah appeared to have been so distressed to have a child that she promised to God that if God answered her prayers, she would bring the child up as a vicar. Her distress was so great that the resident vicar thought she was "mad" and having a depressive relapse. (1 Samuel)

In Samson's case, it is always clear in his mind that it is God he served, not other kinds, rulers or lovers. His life account is full of ethical and moral controversies bordering on the saying "it didn't say that"; for example, the entire book of Samson centres on sharing his sleeping hours with Delilah out of passion rather than respectful love and duty. (Judges 13-16)

The denial

Sections of the church assert that the role of Christians in the world is exclusively spiritual – we are saved unto eternity (e.g., the "glory" in 2 Thessalonians 2:14), and we are in the world and not of the world. (John 17:14-15) They are usually called the "Evangelicals": a fitting designation because we want to evangelise everyone about God's grace to save us.

The trouble is that some of us deny any role in other aspects of humanity apart from the spiritual. We leave the poor to the charity, the sick to the hospital, the depressed to the psychiatric nurse, which together suggests we do little if at all for the retiring ministers and pastors, doctors and nurses, and the war veterans who have exhausted their mental, emotional and physical faculties to help others.

This is the Evangelical denial of the whole person. (see also Petersen, 2017; Smith, 2020) Of course, on the other end, we could be spending so much energy and time doing social and humanitarian work that we put God aside more and more regularly to the extent that we are operating as if God does not matter or care. However, the "Evangelical denial" is damaging to the growth of our faith, too.

Let's begin with Jesus: he stated his mission (Luke 4:14-21) as:

What?	Good news
To?	Poor
	Detained (physical, mental, spiritual, etc.)
	Blind
	Oppressed

Figure 1 Jesus' mission in a nutshell

I consider it God's grace that I grew up being aware of some aspects of mental health struggles. Accepting clinical, medical and behavioural intervention does not go against our faith; secondly, it is complementary. (Mark 5:35-43)(Lloyd-Jones, n.d.) Prayer and spiritual discipline are essential: for the young, the sick, and the elderly, we won't stop them from taking medication or exercising to build up their strength. Our central message should be that Jesus has saved us from spiritual bondage ("Evangelical" emphasis), that we meet with the physical and mental needs of the world in the same way Jesus has healed us, for eternal glory ("Pentecostal" emphasis).

In Mark 14:3-9, we find that Jesus said this, "For you always have the poor with you, but you will not always have me." (Mark 14:3-9) We might take this to mean that Jesus would depart from those we were speaking to, and they needed to decide about their faith. For us who are not contemporaries of Jesus, it can also mean we must not delay believing in Jesus.

But there is more to this verse than it seems.

The above record of what Jesus said, he quoted from Deuteronomy 15:11: "Since there will never cease to be some in need on the earth, I therefore command you, 'Open your hand to the poor and needy neighbour in your land.'" This is taken to mean that we should do our best to attend to those in poverty because the need is so great that we can never fully provide for everyone all the time. Theoharis (Christian Aid, 2025) discussed this further and asserted that we must not forget Deuteronomy

15:4: "There will, however, be no one in need among you, because the Lord is sure to bless you in the land that the Lord your God is giving you as a possession to occupy".

Together, it says that God's kingdom is free of needs, but due to humans' sins, needs remain, i.e. equality and equity are lost.[3] Our salvation through Jesus and his grace is from the bondage of sin (this sentence has an "Evangelical" overtone), which means the totality of spiritual, physical and mental aspects of who we are. "Some view mental illness as a purely spiritual issue and deny the need for medication or other forms of treatment. Others view it as an illness with no spiritual aspect. I believe it's a combination of both." (Sheila Walsh: Petersen, 2017) To assert further, we are "partakers" of the divine nature (2 Peter 1:5). It is notable that the man recorded in Luke 8:26-39 pleaded with Jesus to follow him. Jesus sent him away: He did that, showing his life had changed, his body was being mended, and his mind was freed.

---

[3] Based on definitions from several dictionaries, equality means that the items being compared have the same attributes, while equity refers to fairness between the items.

Mind over actions

Was Samson unable to control himself, for example, to distance himself from Delilah? (Judges 16) He controlled his mind to stay faithful to God's promise so that he would always have superhero strength. In parallel with this knowledge and obedience, he disobeyed the spirit of the law of cleanliness of the time. Arguably, he did not violate the law: no law that said if God had blessed you with the strength of ten giants, then you cannot share a dwelling with a woman not your relative over a few hours, day or night. He sought God's mercy, killed the enemies in one sweep, and died along with them.

No one is too far from God's mercy. How bad can things be? Samson was, in fact, a judge at the time. (Judges 13:5; 24-25) It is a judge dissimilar to what we know today. A judge during biblical times held almost supernatural power (or was licensed to call on some) to rule over everyone on any matter, religious or otherwise. They have been known to summon wars and effect peace treaties.

Did Samson suffer from any depression? The Bible does not say.[4] A clue is that when he was brought out of jail and his enemies demanded that he entertain them, he did so. Most English translations agreed on the description that he "entertained". Checking on the text's original meaning, as best as possible, suggests not only the absence of a classical piano solo concert featuring Mozart (other names available) but also that the entertainment drew further mockery and jest to himself.

The Grace Moment

Whether Samson continued his faith in prison, again, the text does not say. What it says is that Samson prayed to God to give him superhero strength one last time. He had the faith to believe that if he filled in the application form to request it, it would be given to him. Similarly, with Hannah, if God answered her prayer with a child, her obedience would not cease but continue

---

[4] The biblical account of Samson tended to tell an "evidential" story rather than what the author or oral tradition thought Samson thought.

by offering the child, Samuel, to work at the local church. In time, Samuel earned the respect of many near and far and commanded many years of peace in his territory. (1 Samuel)

We might identify more with Hannah than with Samson because she was more "ordinary" than superhuman Samson. However, some of us also see similarities between Samson and Newton's early life. Perhaps a time will come when there is a time of realisation – the "Grace moment" - that our words, thoughts and actions have always been in God's care.

We stop thinking that we are living a life on some independent channel unrelated to what God is doing: God has no interest in us, and we cannot get God's attention. Not so.

There are times, minutes, days, and years when we think God is absent in our lives because we believe he is not interested, we could not fit him in our 24x7x52 schedule, or both, or there was a miscommunication between us.

No more of such thinking: God cares all the time.

God's grace is for everyone.

Are we ready to accept God's grace in our deepest despair?

More thoughts indeed. It's not that simple. Sometimes, even when a helicopter is sending down the rescue basket, we want to be the last to be winched up. No, we don't even want to be on it. We might be in a bad situation; we cannot be helped. No one could extend a helping us. If they do, it's not right to accept it.

Why is there this kind of refusal to receive help?

There is no turning away from the fact that some situations deserve little help. However, we don't wish another person to go through what we have gone through. Also, help is available to make our lives far better going forward. To stay in our state of despair helps no one.

It is also true that we cannot turn around unless part of that package is to repay, recompense, forgive, restore, or, in some other way, repair the damage we have done to others. Accepting God's grace does not mean we can walk away from such "cost". In fact, God's grace is the strength for us to begin that journey to reconcile with those we wronged and ourselves.

Is it fair?

Is it fair that massive panic attacks hit me or a loved one?

Charles Spurgeon was a famous preacher of the late 19th century. (The Editors of Encyclopaedia Britannica, 2018; Hawkes, 2024; Reeves, 2018; The Spurgeon Centre, 2017) He drew many to his sermons. Yet, he suffered from depression. From one tragedy to another, stress and physical pain, he was fully aware of his struggling mental state. He made significant changes to his life to cope with the condition. He sought God to turn his suffering into something positive to help others.

Sheila Walsh (Klett, 2018; Petersen, 2017) exhorts us to be wise in dealing with guilt and shame. The former is about our action; the latter is about us. Both are bad, but for many, the worst realisation is about "us". Hospitalised with severe clinical depression, and fearful about treatment when her dad died in similar circumstances, she later exerted that talking about depression in church "doesn't make it more real or powerful; it brings it out of the shadows into the light and love of Christ ... I can focus on what's broken and wonder where God is or I can sit in the companionship of Christ who suffered for us and worship him in the middle of the mess. That gives my pain meaning and context."

"I arrived at my church office on a beautiful spring morning in May [...] Suddenly, for no perceivable reason, I felt a physical panic begin to well up inside me. My entire body felt like it was on fire." Kirby Smith's (2020) account was thorough and honest. I can relate to what he went through. Depression can affect anyone at any time, and we in the church ought to offer emotional and practical support, too.

Tommy Nelson, a pastor of a megachurch in Texas, encouraged his congregants to meditate on the Bible in dealing with anxiety. That's until Nelson "slipped ... into an emotional hold". In 2018, he held a conference, "The Journey Through Depression and Anxiety", to widen conversations about mental health guidance using "biblical principles and practical truth". (Blair, 2018; The Hub, 2018)

The answer to "Is it fair?" is yours to make. For those suffering, at some point, this thought does come. For those offering care and help, this question can come across as irrelevant and disturbing because no matter how we deal with it, this individual is unique. There is a philosophical question: "fair in comparison to what?" The disturbing aspect stems from the fact that individuals need help and support. We do our best to care, but "fairness" is the wrong way to think about care.

Hearing voices and multiple selves

Depression might not be a suffering condition with the kind of emotional trauma and inhumane treatment that causes another person to die (murder, manslaughter, negligence, etc). But we will feel the experience we have gone through is as bad as a life lost. Some of us would not forgive ourselves for having negative thoughts about ourselves or another person. These are real conditions we face. We can reason that these are only in our thoughts, not real; they represent the thoughts we have consciously chosen to entertain. By refraining from such thinking, we can improve our well-being.

That might be a logical stance, but it shows a lack of understanding about mental trauma and depression. Suffering from such a condition means we become very aware of our "voices". These can feel like an inner voice or what our body tells us in response to something.

The inner voice might be described as our "inner person." This is further explained in the book "Games of Masquerade and Walls of Doubt" (Wong, 2025). The inner person is the invisible person that no other person relates to except the "physical" person. Described this way, the physical person is an equally tricky concept.

But this difficulty is the beginning of a realisation that the different "persons" of an individual are more than our physical aspects.

When we talk to ourselves, we are conversing with this inner person. (Wong, 2025, p. 62) For example, when we convince ourselves that going shopping the next day is a low risk in missing that item, it's talking with the inner person (the example on pg. 7). Even if sufferers agree that some of the negative voices we receive are not ethical or even legal, the real struggle is the persistent nature of such a voice.

It is also important to note that the "voices" might not be what we mean by "voices". These "voices" could represent thoughts and ideas so harmful that we perceive them as if they were spoken aloud. Their influence can be so strong that we find it difficult to dismiss them. Additionally, their impact may resemble a relentless communication system, where the frequency and intensity of the messages can become overwhelming. For example, I remind myself to check my work email every few minutes because I fear receiving a negative message. This builds up my anxiety about responding to negative messages in my inbox.

We can also lecture ourselves about how thoughts are purely imaginative when the factors that lead to a colleague sending a negative message are unfounded. But we are all bound up by thoughts and thoughts of thoughts that render us very tired.

This can also explain why people with mental health issues might be seen to be extraordinarily restless or quiet for an extended period and, in the end, have not achieved anything. The last sentence demonstrates how others view us. It is our daily, hourly, and continuous struggle to battle such thoughts.

The essence of grace

I experienced two bouts of depression. The first descended to me like a wall of gloom. During the recovery phase, I was thankful to God for the way he guided me through previous encounters with anxiety. A year after my recovery, my employer underwent an internal restructuring, which was good and bad for me. The good was continual employment in a new role. The bad was that a whole package of clash of something I still don't understand, but the outcome was increased anxiety levels. (Wong, 2025, pp. 150-60) Leading to my second breakdown was the heightened awareness that my body was showing many symptoms of putting up some defence against something. I had many recurrences of skin rashes.

Throughout the year, I can recall only about five days when I woke up feeling as rested as I should have. This suggests that my biological and physiological systems struggle to cope with significant tension. After a major incident occurred, I decided it was time to consult my general practitioner, who confirmed that I was experiencing a relapse.

The second relapse was not as severe as the first, but during this time, I became increasingly aware of the "voices" conveying both positive and negative messages to me. Additionally, I recognised that I was unable to halt or diminish these messages. Does my experience resonate with you?

Then, what is the essence of God's grace? It is that the healing is happening in me. It has not reached the end, and I am not completely cured. "Grace is actively and continually working in the lives of God's people."[5]

My focus is that I am okay (on balance, all things considered). That means, despite my struggles with sleep, frequent moments of anxiety throughout the day, and the internal conflict regarding my behaviour in social contexts, I have managed to avoid inflicting significant harm on myself or others.

Also, my faith is strong because he enables me to hang on to him. To say, on balance, I feel ok is an understatement. My episodes of anxiety and uncertainty in social situations often

---

[5] https://www.gotquestions.org/definition-of-grace.html

escalate beyond their actual significance. While I may not consciously dwell on these scenarios, I am aware that my subconscious mind is engaged in a complex array of "what if" scenarios in anticipation of upcoming social interactions.

This could be a phone call or online chat, a visit to the shop, travelling to another place, or some other activities beyond the home. My subconscious part has begun building up a myriad of defences given unfamiliar or unpredictable situations.

The essence of grace is that it is grace. It does not force itself into your life. It does not want to win the argument that it is vital in your life. It wants to hear everything you tell it: past histories, your wishes, etc. It wants you to be yourself and to do your best in all situations.

When you allow grace in your life, the transformation it gives is beyond the world. What does that mean? "Beyond the world" means something that cannot be fully described using words and analogies from within our world. Supernatural? Maybe. Godly? That's more likely.

Who is grace?

A life of extreme

King David led a life of trouble: he became a king at a very young age but then spent decades playing cat-and-mouse with King Saul. (1 Samuel 16; 24) He wrote some of the best psalms of devotion to God, yet he followed his lust all the way to murder. At every turn, he repented and sought forgiveness from God.

> O Lord, you brought my soul up from [the grave],
>
> restored me to life from among those gone down to the Pit (Psalm 30:3)
>
> You desire truth in the inward being;
>   therefore teach me wisdom in my secret heart.
> Purge me with hyssop, and I shall be clean;
>   wash me, and I shall be whiter than snow.
> Let me hear joy and gladness;
>   let the bones that you have crushed rejoice.
> Hide your face from my sins,
>   and blot out all my iniquities. (Psalm 51:6-9)

David wrote the following in Psalm 121. When he said about a foot being moved, if we think that was being figurative (e.g., to mean that God will help him to be decisive), I think we are missing the point of this psalm.

> He [God] will not let your foot be moved;
>   he who keeps you will not slumber.
> The sun shall not strike you by day,
>   nor the moon by night. (Ps. 121:3-4)

Further, God knows the rights and wrongs of David. David knows that he is God's appointed. The sun and moon are the witnesses possessing a comprehensive record of all events since the beginning of time. As much as stating a promise and the promise being received (i.e. multiple "voices"), David affirmed God's protection even in the most inconsequential things - the coming and going, or a less archaic version, "what's up?":

> The Lord will keep you from all evil;
>   he will keep your life.
> The Lord will keep
>   your going out and your coming in
>   from this time on and for evermore.
> (Ps. 121:7-8)

A troubled mind

Perhaps a less familiar account than the above about David is that of Cain and Abel. (Genesis 4) Whether it is a case of "equality" missed, or "equity" trashed between the two brothers, the account stated that God had a lesson for Cain.

The crux of this account is that Cain murdered Abel in broad daylight (it must be, because they were in a field).

To succumb to such rage could have started from periods of dark mood, growing into a state of vengeance. I speculate that when Cain responded to God, "My punishment is greater than I can bear!" he was in a dangerous and despairing state of mind. (Genesis 4:13) It's not clear he was sorry or repented. But he seemed to have come from one period of depression (because of the brother, and God) into another (without both the brother and God).

In Cain, we find a person who struggled with a state of mind where he seemed to have always chosen the wrong path in life. The warning from God had no effect on him. God cast him out into the world, and he led a life as a wanderer. God also made a "mark" on him such that no one would cause harm to him. God's grace remained on Cain; he would not suffer further consequences from his murder. (Genesis 4:15-16)

Since there is no further account about him after this, we can hold on to the suggestion that Cain is someone struggling with a troubled state of mind all his life. He sounded like someone who acts on impulse and unchecked raw feelings. For example, if he cannot acquire something, he will kill whoever has that item to get it. The totality of God's grace was available to him, but he chose not to receive it.

If I could decide

The family situation in Abraham's household is complex to the extreme. (Various chapters from Genesis 11 to 25) How much this resembles relationships in our community is for us to reflect, though no one is likely to refute that the account cannot be truthful. The story about Hagar begins in Genesis 16 and continues in Genesis 21, with another mention of her in Genesis 25.

Abraham is the one who should focus our attention because he appears to have very little room in his decisions and actions in response to Sarah and Hagar. But no, I want to focus on Hagar. How much Hagar had a choice in what happened to her is up for debate. When Abraham sent Hagar and the newly born Ishmael away, a new period of the lives of mother and son opened one of total freedom. (Genesis 21)

There appears to be more negligence on the part of Abraham on Hagar than the latter suddenly finding herself having to make every decision for her and the boy. While Abraham did prepare Hagar and his son thoroughly for the trip, the shadows of negligence loom over his preparations because there was no one he was sending them to,[6] no destination, and no safety measures to shield them from the perils of the "road". (Genesis 21:14) Hagar went from a crowded environment with no room to be herself to another environment without room for decision-making. If not a desert, it is a flat plain, a lifeless place.[7]

---

[6] For various anthropological factors, even before the days of email, relevant communication is done, and any possible arrangement confirmed, so that visitors to a new place are well received.

[7] Speaking of safety protection, it is possible that Hagar went (or has been instructed to go) in a certain direction or area where no one else would go.

If she could decide, she would likely return to Abraham and Sarah. The fact that she did not do so painted a condition where to die is better than to live. It looked like she could not think of any outcome apart from the boy dying. The account said she "lifted her voice and wept". However, commentators reminded us that it was the boy's voice that caught God's attention, who then consoled Hagar. (21:16-17)

We can imagine some aspects of Abraham's household at this time. Given that we rely on a written version of the account first made more than two thousand years ago, and that was based on generations of oral history (which might be another thousand years), and then our version of the scripture was product of several translation attempts, some of the details and nuances have been lost. Alternative versions of some accounts are available to readers and scholars alike, and they have aided scribes, ancient and modern, in making the best decisions on words and meanings.

The implication of Hagar's story from the text, reinforced a little by scholars, is that she appeared to conduct herself with less restraint than others hoped she would. That does not mean she was immoral, irresponsible and careless. However (my speculation number 2), Sarah might be a more "cultured" person. Despite her faith and that of Abraham, she still could not conceive. The two were not getting on well because of that (speculation number 3). Anything else would have been seen to be more "relaxed" and carefree than what's going on between Abraham and Sarah. One day, Sarah took offence when she noticed Ishmael laughing and mocking her son, Isaac. (Genesis 21:9) That was probably a situation no one could handle. There is no doubt what the text says: if these are adults, this could be what Moses faced, where insults led to argument and death. (Exodus 2:11-15) Whether there is room to realise an offset of "equality" or "equity" is impossible to know; for example, one child could have inadvertently made the other one angry, and a mother would protect her child first.

Further, it also seems that Hagar was not thankful and gracious enough for being in that household. The son, found laughing and mocking (Isaac), might point to what he learned from his mother. This is viewed from one perspective, where Hagar remained a servant.

It is easier for us today to say Hagar ought to decide to bring him up in a respectable manner in the household and sever expectations from her community. However, we would have missed the challenging issues Hagar continued to face. [8] The extensive accounts of warlords, princes, kings, pharaohs, and judges in the scriptures tell us about a complex social world not dissimilar from our own.

Going forward

Here are some questions to discuss in groups to support individuals with mental health issues or concerns. This might be useful for a church or other similar groups.

✝   What examples have we come across of people in our group who might be suffering from mental health issues?

---

[8] This reminds me of the account of Daniel: he continued to perform his prayer rituals even when that had become illegal. The reason we know that detail was likely because the author was telling the story in Daniel's favour. The nature of the two accounts is very different and putting them side by side is a dangerous exercise. However, there is something here about oral tradition and authorship (or scribe-ship) that could have influenced our reading.

✝ What kinds of issues did they face? What help did they receive? Did they improve with the help?

✝ Imagine a group where we don't have or are not aware of anyone battling with anxiety all the time. How important is it that we welcome such visitors? Why? What would we do if they attended our events, worship or activities?

✝ Someone in our group has become quieter and quieter in recent months, missing some events when they never missed any. What conversations would we have with this person to find out more about whether they have personal concerns?

✝ Imagine we attend the weekly prayer meeting. Hilary discloses details about Jo's depression conditions when Jo is not present at the meeting. Others think Hilary has gone too far without Jo's permission. What should we do?

✝ Mo says their son Bartholomew is diagnosed with depressive mood. He remains busy and enjoys a range of activities but is seeking help for his depression. Sam, a mental health nurse, is in the group. Sam, who is too busy with work to care for Ba, is open to other suggestions to help. Discuss your suggestions with Sam / Ba / Mo in your group.

✝   Elijah obeyed God and was successful in revealing the truth of God. (1 Kings 18:36-39). Soon after that, he was running for his life, getting very depressed when he cried to God, "I am the only one left, and now they are trying to kill me too" (1 Kings 19:14). What else did he say? See e.g. 1 Kings 19:4-5.

✝   1 Kings 19:11-13. How did Elijah recognise it when God appeared to him?

✝   Then, back to "business as usual", God gave Elijah further instructions: see 1 Kings 19:15-18. What else do we learn in these verses?

✝   What else do the verses 1 Kings 19:3-9 tell us about God's provision for people like Elijah?

✝   Recall how God helped us in complicated situations. Write or tell others what happened in the style of Elijah.

✝   Luke 8:26-39 is another passage that is difficult to read because of unusual things. What does this passage tell us about this person's trouble before Jesus came to him?

✝   Instead of running away, this person came to Jesus (we know that because he was at Jesus's feet) and spoke with high levels of emotion (he shouted at point-blank distance). How might "grace in depression" be relevant for this person?

✝   Adam, Eve and Cain are aware of their predicament due to their sinful nature, and they acknowledge God; however, their description in the scriptures suggests a lack of remorse and repentance. (Genesis 3-4) Were these individuals beyond God's grace?

✝   We might regard our words, deeds, and thoughts as serious as this person's condition or worse. Deep down, we want to be rescued (see the rescue fiction on pg. 16). How should we respond to people struggling with mental health conditions?

✝   There is a story that tells of a guy who severed ties with his family due to a lack of grace for him, the older brother who complained about a lack of grace for him when his brother "changed his mind" having lost all monies, and came home, and their father who had a mental crisis of a different kind that led to him to throw a party of unceasingly gracious proportions. What story is this, and what lessons might there be about dealing with mental health issues?

✝ Read Ruth 1:19-21 about two ladies in respective personal crises, having to make a decision that would determine the rest of their lives. How did Naomi describe herself?

✝ Read Ruth 4:13-22. What happened to Naomi and Ruth?

✝ Peter experienced a horrific crisis: he broke down because he failed himself and Jesus. See Luke 22.

✝ Read Matthew 26 and 27 and focus on Judas Iscariot. What are the differences between Peter and Judas in dealing with a life-threatening personal crisis?

What about church?

At some stage, we need to address the question of being a church that is aware of the need to care for those suffering from depression. That is a very long statement of an attribute. I try to avoid saying "depressive friendly" or similar because that kind of labelling does not go far enough.

Here is an analogy about relevance. A committee consisting of people from the villages is created. The objective of the committee is to improve bus shelters adjacent to nightclubs. Even if all the committee members intrinsically know the need for improvement, the main problem is the absence of representation from folks in the city.

Discussion about what a church should be is always a complex topic, exacerbated during the COVID-19 lockdown when, for months, we could not meet in person. (For further readings, see Mann and Wong, 2020; 2021). Having denominational labels is terrible enough.

I believe the starting point is that the church is extensive in people. In that sense, it is a church with all types of people who regularly attend its services, events, etc. With their regular attendance at church activities, we are in a good position to help and support them. No, that's the <u>wrong</u> approach: It is true that we can use the "Chicken or egg" analogy to explain the fact that we can't deal with what support we can provide until the people are here or regularly attending.

The fact that other approaches are complicated does not make the "egg first" (or is it "chicken first"?) approach right. The point is that applying our "open door policy" means we take the "open door"[9] to the people where they are. Many of us can attribute the beginning of our faith journey to attending a church, soup kitchen, fellowship, Christian Union, Bible Study or similar activities. These organisations did not exist based on knowing how many new people would come in the next few months of opening and how many new souls would be saved. We have come through that journey. We came to faith when others exercised their faith in setting up the church that met our needs.

---

[9] Not to be confused with Open Doors International https://opendoors.org that began with delivering Bibles to persecuted people who need them, extending to humanitarian efforts too.

A common approach in church planting is setting up that community with people from that community. The talents will come along with offers to help, as will the needs and challenges. Using the "village for city" analogy above (pg. 37), we want to avoid putting down too much of the wrong, or incompatible, kind of "feeling" about this new community of faith. Incompatible with whom? For a start, incompatible with those suffering from mental health issues.

From our eye contact to involving participation, we need to do and be the type of person who conveys the comfort of welcome. What this means is a challenge to describe. Using another analogy, instead of coming to church, Jesus took the church with him to encounter the "demon-possessed" man. We imagine that he spoke very sternly to this person (in response to him screaming at him), but it's unclear from the text that this is the case.

"Absence speaks volumes" might be a fitting description for Mary, Jesus's mother. The first moment of great reflection was probably when the shepherds visited them in the manger: "But Mary treasured up all these things and pondered them in her heart" (Luke 2:19).

Of course, on its own, this does not make Mary suffer from depression. What catches my attention is her "pondering". We won't debate any difference between pondering in the "heart" and "mind." Pondering suggests holding on to some thoughts over time. It is not the same as meditation, which focuses on a thought or idea to help with relaxation (broadly speaking). Also different from pondering is questioning or discussing, which includes taking different perspectives and perhaps validating the concept.

Pondering is an intentional search for direction and meaning from a given idea. In Mary's case, without over-dramatising, this could be the first moment in weeks or months she could sit still or could not move more than 3 metres without needing assistance or protection. The visits from the shepherds posed a confirmation more than a surprise to Mary.

Pondering is like when I first got a job offer based solely on my merit: my thought was that this could be God's plan for me, the first chapter unfolding. It is my part to exercise faith to stay the course.

As noted above, it is not (or not likely) that Mary suffered from anxiety or a mental breakdown. She didn't experience that when the angel appeared to her and offloaded what sounded like an empire-building plan in an embryonic form, with no clue on the next step. Having to adhere to ever-changing legal requirements and travel a journey of 4 to 5 days of some 120km is a tremendous toll for many, whether physical or mental, let alone with a newborn. (Matthew 2)

Pondering must have been there and about when Mary remarks to the servants at Cana, "Do whatever he tells you" (John 2:5). This follows a mother-son conversation, a window to their relationship. Far from getting depressed, pressing for a "discussion", or moving away for a period of meditation, she acted knowing and expecting Jesus would do what he thought right and timely. Whether it was the "right hour" for Jesus, he did do something, turning water into wine, in the course of which he reversed the cultural practice of having the best wine first.

There were scant records of Mary after this until the death and resurrection of Jesus. (Mark 16:1; John 19:25; Acts 1:14) Mary's "pondering" is a healthy state of mind, rooted in a soul submitted to the will of God. Rid we are from our mind of how "holy" Mary was, let alone the influence of "artists" who could well have "passed on" their own ethical and cultural manifestations to the person they evolved through their brushes. In other words, Mary could be as ordinary as the screaming kids helping each other to chocolate while enlarging a sandcastle (apply our own imagination).

The only thing unusual with the manger is not the halo over Mary's head, or having the right kind of animal smell leading to Joseph debating which corner shops would have the right brand of baby milk, but that the shepherds left their sheep (or some came along) and were allowed into rows of terraces: they were at the wrong place at the wrong time.

Depression can affect anyone. Crucially, it is how we manage it that counts. Jesus led such a busy life, and the scriptures have no record of his human mental state. We can speculate that when he faced extremely personally challenging situations (e.g., the death of his close friend Lazarus, John 11), he would experience turmoil as a person. Further, there is mention of "his sweat was like drops of blood falling to the ground" (Luke 22:44). Scholars do not deny the possibility that the blood could be real. Jesus' struggle was not a personal tragedy, or to stay the course to obey his father's will to the end. The weight of the sins of the world could have been the burden Jesus took on, which made the task so much more challenging. Again, the challenge was not so much to choose between proceeding (obedience to God) or not, but that the weight of humans' sins was so great.

Samson assured himself that his state of mind was sound. He and David allowed themselves into things that are not pleasing to God. Not much has changed since the days of Adam and Eve.

Samuel's sons were disastrous judges (1 Samuel 8), but he remained faithful and obedient to God all his life. Few may know about Noah's binge drinking habit. (Genesis 9) But we know that God has also enabled him to be a one-of-a-kind, top-of-the-mountain, ocean-going cruise builder, and absolute faith and obedience to God to see through such an empire-building plan, effected by all animals two-by-two and the ensuing dry-safari-on-water. (Genesis 6-8)

Having negotiated with God for a son, Hannah obeyed God in giving Samuel for God's use. She might have experienced great anxiety in not having a child, yet it is her faith in God that made her so remarkable and the mother of one of the most excellent judges.

Abigail kept her faith despite a personal tragedy in marriage. (1 Samuel 25) Rahab probably did not have much choice in life. When she realised God had come to her, she responded positively. (Joshua 2, 6) Hagar (pg. 29) was recorded as giving God a name "El-roi" (Genesis 16:13), which means "God of seeing" or "God who sees". The incident was when she ran away from Abraham and Sarah, the latter having mistreated her. So sanguine was Hagar she wanted to remember it was an angel that found her near a spring of water; it was named Beer-lahai-roi, meaning "well of the living one who sees me". (Genesis 16:14)

Remember another detail in Elijah's story. A widow was going to have her last meal with her son since there was nothing else to sustain them. To make matters worse, Elijah had requested that this lady make a meal for him. After stating the obvious, Elijah explained what God would do. She obeyed, and the food she made lasted for several days. Not only that, but Elijah also healed her son. Her faith grew from strength to strength. (1 Kings 17)

Unfortunately, apart from "widow", there is no record of this lady's name to whom Elijah outstretched. The severity of life might resemble some of what happened to us – zero contract work, but too competitive, money is not forthcoming, no food, no shelter, and no friends or anyone I could call on to hear my story. What is more important is that God takes the "open door" to where people are.

That does not mean giving up on having a building for our group. We will need one for corporate worship and a central place with facilities for recurring activities. This is the subject of our book "Worship in Cyber Church: Buildings & Missions". (Mann and Wong, 2024) In being mission-focused, the building takes on spiritual meanings.

Open door church

Let's keep the grammatically erroneous description "Open Door Church". Consider the following:

✝ Who are the people we should take our church's "open doors" to?

✝   There is a lady in the New Testament who came to accept Jesus as her Saviour and then opened her home for church use. See Acts 16:13-15. What else can we find out?

✝   Someone asked, "I come to church to worship God, not to do things like the Open Door project. When do we have the doxology? What will we do about the candles and windows? Bell ringers and choirs, once they are stopped, we will lose them forever." What might be a suitable response?

✝   In what ways can a "church without walls"[10] work where we live?

✝   One of the groups said their lunchtime "Open Door" session at work has a positive outcome, and they wanted more materials on positive thinking in dealing with mental health. What might we suggest?

---

[10] "About us", http://tinyurl.com/cyberchurch8280; also (Mann and Wong, 2024, p. 7)

✝   A group has two ideas:

(a) run a mental health awareness table at the supermarket to have as many conversations with shoppers as possible, and

(b) hand out a mental health information leaflet to invite people to contact us with their mental health needs so we can follow up.

In both cases, we have enough experts available to respond with help and support for all individuals. Both will run two or three times a week for over 4 months.

Discuss whether (a) or (b) is a better choice in our group, or suggest modifications to one of them.

✝   "Our 'Open Door' activity has not worked. People do come to sports activities, but they are not interested in talking about stress, mental health, anxiety, etc., even though some of them are suffering from it." The group that sent you this message will meet with you for a regular badminton game. This time, they have 5 minutes to talk about the message. Discuss what questions you want to ask them to help them decide what to do next with their Open Door.

✝   What might be some good ideas to include elements of Sunday service in an Open Door activity?

✝   As above, include an Open Door activity in a Sunday service?

✝   "Open Door" takes much effort since each event requires detailed planning. Discuss what could make this more manageable.

✝   After investigation, a group concludes that "Open Door" will fail where they are because of a lack of social and neutral space to meet; where people do meet, they do so in one of the churches. One idea is to have Open Door introductions at their events so that people know about it and can seek help. What might be the challenges with this arrangement? What might be other ideas?

✝   Those who are in primary schools are excited about holding Open Door activities because many of their friends are bored at home. Our group will mentor them and help them develop a schedule so that at the end of 10 weeks, they can say who has enjoyed their activities. List five items to ask them: we must have their answers before further discussions.

✝   "They keep getting into trouble because they don't have friends." What should we consider when including this concern in our Open Door Church?

✝   From 20 regulars, now down to 4. We can only sustain a monthly activity. What should we do to close this Open Door?

An "Open Door Church" takes some thinking since it is something new to the core of what a church should be. The "home fellowship" was the early church's practical extension and growth. The different formats of the church come about through many changes over centuries. The needs have also changed, beginning as a sect of Judaism, then as a rejected and persecuted group on the run as far as West Asia and North Africa - much of "what is a church" was forgotten, which made it relatively easier to set up new things.

One trend in the very short outline of "church history" above is that accounts of people saved by God are more difficult to find than those of church buildings, the resurgence or demise of denominations, and clergy. To take on "Open Door Church" is another wedge that allows more distractions our way.

I say the above because it is my struggle. Years of preparation as a musician and much work done in worship are not usable in Open Door Church unless it has a "worship" element. As set out in the "Buildings and Missions", we are reminded that the church is not brick and mortar. (Mann and Wong, 2024) It is about people connecting to encourage, admonish and grow together. The building is crucial as it shelters us and is convenient for our identity, storage and events. But it does not determine our life; it is the reverse.

Some in church did not want to hear about my struggle dealing with anxiety and the broader context. It takes a lot of listening; there is no easy fix. Others in church have responded unconditionally when listening to my account, showing prayerful understanding.

Yet, the structure is in the way. In comparison, I could message my GP for my medication, and it is done. The point here is that the church needs to be flexible to allow people with different ways to sound out their problems to anyone and connect with anyone they choose, rather than being restricted to when we have our worship services, because we cannot expect anyone to have time on other days.

Your turn

In concluding this book, I'd like to encourage readers to continue "pondering" in what ways God is healing us to cope or recover from mental health issues. In Christian Aid's Act on Poverty study materials, one topic was "Hopeful". (Christian Aid, 2025) It reminded us that Jesus' mission was to save individuals from oppression. This means our souls, but also our physical and mental needs.

There are many other topics concerning "Open Door Church". Messy church and Café church are two ideas. It might be an added challenge when this is developed alongside existing worship services. Another approach might be to have an associated group of people not involved in existing services, tasks, etc.

We often focus on problems first. That is natural as humans, and we don't want to go too far when problems stop the project altogether. What greatly helps is that we think outside of church and church services and focus on the community's needs. If the list of needs is about the same length as the outstanding tasks in the church, we don't know our community that well.[11]

The New Testament is an account of the early church. Very few churches today model their worship life fully on the early church and are successful. The early church had its specific context, particularly the early attempts of all things about the church, from doctrine to roles. It is not that issues of the NT church are not applicable for us today, but that we need God's wisdom to meditate on the way God was relevant to the NT folks and us two thousand years later, and to speak about and take action on God's grace in many lives in poverty.

---

[11] And if the list is really that short, it means we are living in a commune where there are no other people apart from church-folk.

References

Blair, L. (2018) *Megachurch pastor Tommy Nelson reveals medication helped him through depression, anxiety.* Available at: https://www.christianpost.com/news/megachurch-pastor-tommy-nelson-reveals-medication-helped-him-through-depression-anxiety.html (Accessed: 14-Aug-2024).

Christian Aid (2025) *Week 5: Hopeful.* Act on Poverty. Christian Aid. Available at: https://www.christianaid.org.uk/get-involved/campaigns/act-poverty-session-five-hopeful (Accessed: 2-Apr-2025).

The Editors of Encyclopaedia Britannica (2018) *C. H. Spurgeon.* Encyclopedia Britannica. Available at: https://www.britannica.com/biography/C-H-Spurgeon (Accessed: 5-Apr-2025).

Hawkes, J. (2024) *Charles Spurgeon on suffering, depression and humour.* Eat, Write, Sleep. Available at: https://www.eatwritesleep.com/2024/04/charles-spurgeon-on-suffering-depression-and-humour/ (Accessed: 2-Apr-2025).

The Hub (2018) *Tommy Nelson - the journey through depression and anxiety.* Available at: https://youtu.be/wjq56VF9Oz8 (Accessed: 14-Aug-2024).

Klett, L. M. (2018) *Sheila Walsh opens up about depression, says church must 'wake up' to 'epidemic' among pastors.* The Christian Post. Available at: https://www.christianpost.com/books/sheila-walsh-depression-church-must-wake-up-epidemic-among-pastors.html (Accessed: 14-Aug-2024).

Lloyd-Jones, M. (n.d.) *Spiritual depression.* MLJ Trust. Available at: https://www.mljtrust.org/sermons/spiritual-depression/spiritual-depression/ (Accessed: 2-Dec-2023).

Mann, P. and Wong, D. T. W. (2020) *Worship in Cyber Church: Challenges, opportunities and debates.* Portsmouth: Compass Publishing.

--- (2021) *Worship in Cyber Church: Blendedness, inclusiveness and discipleship.* Portsmouth: Compass Publishing.

--- (2024) *Worship in Cyber Church: Buildings & missions.* London: Erleigh Publishing.

Petersen, J. (2017) *Christian faith and mental health: an interview with Sheila Walsh.* Bible Gateway. Available at: https://www.biblegateway.com/blog/2017/11/christian-faith-and-mental-health-an-interview-with-sheila-walsh/ (Accessed: 14-Aug-2024).

Reeves, M. (2018) *Did you know that Charles Spurgeon struggled with depression?* Crossway. Available at: https://www.crossway.org/articles/did-you-know-that-charles-spurgeon-struggled-with-depression/ (Accessed: 8-Feb-2024).

Smith, K. (2020) *I was a pastor struggling with depression. The Evangelical community offered virtually no helpful resources.* Baptist News Global. Available at: https://baptistnews.com/article/i-was-a-pastor-struggling-with-depression-the-evangelical-community-offered-virtually-no-helpful-resources/ (Accessed: 4-Nov-2023).

The Spurgeon Centre (2017) *11 reasons Spurgeon was depressed.* The Spurgeon Centre. Available at: https://www.spurgeon.org/resource-library/blog-entries/11-reasons-spurgeon-was-depressed/ (Accessed: 12-11-2023).

Wong, D. T. W. (2025) *Games of masquerade and walls of doubt. People, systems and mental health at a London university.* London: Fountain Framework Publishing.

www.ingramcontent.com/pod-product-compliance
Lightning Source LLC
Chambersburg PA
CBHW060033040426
42333CB00042B/2433